QUALIT
OF RIGHTEOUS
PEOPLE

Prof Javed Iqbal Saani

**PhD (CS), MBA (MIS), MBA (Finance), BBA
(Bus Admin)**

Intellectual Capital Enterprise
Limited, London

ISBN-13 : 978-1089864585

Library Classification:
Religious>Islam>General

Published by Intellectual Capital Enterprise Limited, ICE Kemp House, 152-160 City Road, London, EC1 V2N.
Printed in England with the collaboration of amazon.co.uk.

CONTENTS

About the author

Javed Iqbal was brought up in Rawalakot (AJ&K). He received his Ph.D. from the University of Salford and an MBA (Information Management) from the University of Hull. Previously Dr. Iqbal received BBA and an MBA (in Finance) from the University of AJ&K both with distinction. The University of Azad Jammu & Kashmir, Muzaffarabad (AJ&K) awarded him two gold medals for his educational performance. The government of Pakistan selected him for higher education and deputed him to the UK to complete his doctorate. The government of Pakistan awarded him $100, 000 for it.

Professor Iqbal joined IQRA University Islamabad campus as an associate professor in 2006. He became the head of Department of Technology Management in International Islamic University

Islamabad (IIUI) in 2012. Dr. Iqbal joined AKU (AJ&K) as a professor in 2015 and has been appointed as a Dean Faculty of Management Sciences.

His article titled "Learning from a Doctoral Research Project: Structure and Content of a Research Proposal" has been ranked by the Deakin University of Australia as the best piece of research for doctoral students. This research paper is widely used and referred to all over the world. Dr. Javed Iqbal has been nominated by an international organization for the Award of Distinguished Scientist for his research contribution. Professor Iqbal has published 22 research articles and 23 books so far. He has developed an interest in Islamic Leadership Style recently. Professor Iqbal has published in such International Journals as *Electronic Journal of Business Research Methods*, *European Journal of Social Sciences*, *Œconomica*, and *European Journal of Scientific Research*. His books on various subjects are available on Amazon, details are at the end of the book.

You can reach him @ iqbalsaani@gmail.com

Value of knowledge

Say (to them, O Muhammad(ﷺ)): Are those who know equal with those who know not? But only men of understanding will pay heed. [Az-Zumar: 9]

Value of knowledge I

Anas (May Allah (SWT) be pleased with him) reported: The Messenger of Allah (SWT) (ﷺ) said, "He who goes forth in search of knowledge is considered as struggling in the Cause of Allah (SWT) until he returns." [At-Tirmidhi].

Abu Hurairah (May Allah (SWT) be pleased with him) reported: Messenger of Allah (SWT) (ﷺ) said, "Verily! The world is accursed and what it contains is accursed, except remembrance of Allah (SWT) and those who associate themselves with Allah (SWT); and a learned man, and a learning person." [At- Tirmidhi, Book 1, Hadith 478

Value of Knowledge II

Abu'd-Darda' (رضي الله عنه) said, "I heard the Messenger of Allah (SWT), (ﷺ), say,

1. 'Allah (SWT) will make the path to the Garden easy for anyone who travels a path in search of knowledge.

2. Angels spread their wings for the seeker of knowledge out of pleasure for what he is doing.

3. Everyone in the heavens and everyone in the earth asks forgiveness for a man of knowledge, even the fish in the water.

4. The superiority of the man of knowledge to the man of worship is like the superiority of the moon to all the planets.

5. The men of knowledge are the heirs of the Prophet (ﷺ)'s.

6. The Prophet (ﷺ)'s bequeath neither dinar nor dirham; they bequeath knowledge. Whoever takes it has taken an ample portion.'"

[Abu Dawud and at-Tirmidhi; Riyadh us Salihin, Hadith 1388, p. 211]

Qualities of good leader/manager

It was by the mercy of God that you were lenient with them (O Muhammad (ﷺ)), for if you had been severe and hard-hearted, they would have forsaken you. So, pardon them and ask (God's) forgiveness for them and consult with them upon the conduct of affairs. [Al-e-Imran: 159]

Hadhrat Ibn 'Umar (رضي الله عنه) reports that Rasulullah (ﷺ) said "Three persons are such as will have no fear of the horrors of the Day of Judgement, nor they will be required to render an account. They will stroll merrily on mounds of musk until the people are relieved of rendering their account. One is a person who learned the Qur'an, merely seeking Allah (SWT)'s pleasure and therewith leads people in salat in a manner that they are pleased with him; the second person is the one who invites men to salaat for the pleasure of Allah (SWT) alone. <u>The third person is the one who has fair dealings between him and his master, as well as between himself and his subordinates</u>" [Quoted by Al-Tibrani in Al-Majam Al-Slaasa; Fazail-e-Amaal, Virtues of the Holy Qur'an, Hadith 36]

Qualities of good leader/manager II

Abdullah ibn-e-'Umar RadiyAllah (SWT)u 'anhuma narrates that a person came to Nabi and asked: O Rasulullah (ﷺ)! How many times may I forgive my servant? Nabi remained silent. <u>The man asked again: O Rasulullah (ﷺ)! How many times may I forgive my servant? He replied: Everyday seventy times.</u> (Tirmidhi) Note: In Arabic, the figure 'seventy' is used to express too many in number. [Muntakhib Ahadith, p. 415]

Allah (SWT), the Exalted

In the name of Allah (SWT), the Beneficent, the Merciful.

1. All that is in the heavens and the earth glorifieth Allah (SWT); and He is the Mighty, the Wise. 2. His is the Sovereignty of the heavens and the earth; He quickeneth and He giveth death, and He can do all things. 3. He is the First and the Last, and the Outward and the Inward, and He is Knower of all things. 4. He is Who created the heavens and the earth in six Days; then He mounted the Throne. He knoweth all that entereth the earth and all that emergeth therefrom and all that cometh down from the sky and all that ascendeth therein, and He is with you wheresoever ye may be. And Allah (SWT) is Seer of what ye do. 5. His is the Sovereignty of the heavens and the earth, and unto Allah (SWT) (all) things are brought back. 6. He causeth the night to pass into the day, and He causeth the day to pass into the night, and He is the knower of all that is in the breasts. [Al-Hadeedh: 1-6]

Dedication

To my parents who invested heavily for our education and remained engaged in prayers for our success and wellbeing.

Acknowledgment

Special gratitude is due to all those who helped me to compile the work. I am also obliged to my family who spared me to embark on the project. They also provide valuable information which enriched the contents of this effort. May Allah (SWT) reward them for their contribution? Ameen!

Preface

All prayers to Allah (SWT), the exalted, slat wa slam to all the Prophet (AS) especially upon the last (ﷺ), mercy and blessings upon his noble companions. May Allah (SWT) bestow upon his forgiveness to the entire ummah and ummah of all the Prophets (AS). And all those who received the right guidance.

The purpose of the book is to find out some qualities of noble people from Quran and Hadith. It is a collection of about 160 ayah and 36 ahadith (including beginning pages). The author has described in detail ten major topics which include ayah and ahadith. Such as believe in Allah (SWT), fear of Allah (SWT), righteousness, relay on Allah (SWT), seeking forgiveness, being patient, being truthful to everyone, asking Devine repentance, remembrance of Allah (SWT) and emigration for the cause of Allah (SWT). Certain surahs describe many qualities together such as [Al-e-Imran, Al-Furqan, Al-Ahzab and Al-Maarij. These have included in the last chapter i.e. forty qualities. The target is myself; I will try to inculcate these qualities in my practices and hope that reader can do the same.

I pray to Allah (SWT), the Exalted, to accept the humble effort and make it a source of forgiveness for me and the entire ummah. May it be a source of guidance for readers. Ameen!

Suggestions are welcome so that the author can incorporate them in the future editions.

Prof Javed Iqbal Saani, Ph.D.

Manchester August 11, 2019

1 BELIEVE IN ALLAH (SWT)

It includes 9 ayah and 3 ahadith.

A-Ayah

Allah (SWT) will not leave the believers in the state in which you are now, until He distinguishes the wicked from the good. Nor will Allah (SWT) disclose to you the secrets of the Ghaib (unseen), but Allah (SWT) chooses of His Messengers whom He pleases. **So, believe in Allah (SWT) and His Messengers.** And if you believe and fear Allah (SWT), then for you there is a great reward. [Ar-Raad: 179]

O you who have believed, **obey** Allah (SWT) and obey the Messenger and those in authority among you. And if you disagree over anything, refer it to Allah (SWT) and the Messenger **if you should believe in Allah (SWT) and the Last Day**. That is the best [way] and best in the result. [An-Nisa: 59]

So those who believe in Allah (SWT) and **hold fast** to Him —He will admit them to mercy from Himself and **bounty** and guide them to Himself on a straight path. [An-Nisa: 175]

And why should we not believe in Allah (SWT) and what has come to us of the truth? And we **aspire** that our Lord will admit us [to Paradise] with the righteous people." [Al-Maidah: 84]

The mosques of Allah (SWT) are only to be maintained by those who **believe in Allah (SWT)** and the **Last Day and establish prayer and give zakah and do not fear except Allah (SWT),** for it is expected that those will be of the [rightly] guided. [At-Tawbah: 18]

Those who believe in Allah (SWT) and the Last Day would **not ask permission of you to be excused from striving [i.e., fighting]** with their wealth and their lives. And Allah (SWT) is Knowing of those who fear Him. [At-Tawbah: 44]

The believers are only those who believe in Allah (SWT) and His Messenger and, **when they are [meeting] with him for a matter of common interest, do not depart until they have asked his permission.**

Indeed, those who ask your permission, [O Muhammad]–those are the ones who believe in Allah (SWT) and His Messenger. So, when they ask your permission for something of their affairs, then give permission to whom you will among them and ask forgiveness for them of Allah (SWT). Indeed, Allah (SWT) is Forgiving and Merciful. [An-Nur: 62]

You will not find a people who believe in Allah (SWT) and the Last Day having affection for those who oppose Allah (SWT) and His Messenger, even if they were their fathers or

their sons or their brothers or their kindred. Those –He has decreed within their hearts faith and supported them with spirit from Him. And We will admit them to gardens beneath which rivers flow, wherein they abide eternally. Allah (SWT) is pleased with them, and they are pleased with Him –those are the party of Allah (SWT). Unquestionably, the party of Allah (SWT) –they are successful. [Al-Mujadilah: 22]

B-Ahadith

1-'Ali narrated that **the Messenger of Allah (SWT) said: 'A slave (of Allah (SWT)) shall not believe until he believes in four: The testimony of La Ilaha IllAllah (SWT), and that I am the Messenger of Allah (SWT) whom He sent with the Truth, and he believes in the death, and he believes in the Resurrection after death, and he believes in Al-Qadar.''** [Jami` at-Tirmidhi, Vol. 4, Book 6, Hadith 2145]

2-Abu Hurairah narrated that **the Messenger of Allah (SWT) said: "Trials will not cease afflicting the believing man and the believing woman in their self, children, and wealth, until they meet Allah (SWT) without having any sin." [Jami` at-Tirmidhi, Vol. 4, Book 10, Hadith 2399]**

3-**It is reported on the authority of Anas that the Messenger of Allah (SWT) (ﷺ) said:** No bondsman believes, and, in the hadith narrated by Abdul Warith, no person believes, till I am dearer to him than the members of his household, his wealth and the whole of mankind. [Sahih Muslim, Book 1, Hadith 70]

Key points

1-Allah (SWT) Commands to believe Allah (SWT)

So, believe in Allah (SWT) and His Messengers. [Ar-Raad: 179]

2-Who believe in Allah (SWT)?

- **Supporters of mosques**. Mosques of Allah (SWT) are only to be maintained[1] (Those who are supporting the mosques, they believe in Allah (SWT)) [At-Tawbah: 18]
- **Establish prayer** [At-Tawbah: 18]
- **Give zakah** [At-Tawbah: 18]
- **Do not fear except Allah (SWT)** [At-Tawbah: 18]
- **Do not make excuses for not striving in the path of Allah (SWT)** would not ask permission of you to be excused from striving [i.e., fighting] [At-Tawbah: 44]
- **Asking Prophet's permission before leaving him**. When they are [meeting] with him for a matter of common interest, do not depart until they have asked his permission. [An-Nur: 62]
- **Love for Allah (SWT)** You will not find a people who believe in Allah (SWT) and the Last

---

[1] Alternative word for it is "Supported"

Day <u>having affection for those who oppose Allah (SWT) and His Messenger, even if they were their fathers or their sons or their brothers or their kindred</u>. [Al-Mujadilah: 22]

- **Do Dua for the paradise.** And why should we not believe in Allah (SWT) and what has come to us of the truth? And we aspire that our Lord will admit us [to Paradise] with the righteous people." [Al-Maidah: 84]

The Messenger of Allah (SWT) said: 'A slave (of Allah (SWT)) shall not believe until he believes in four:

- The testimony of La Ilaha IllAllah (SWT), and
- That I am the Messenger of Allah (SWT) whom He sent with the Truth,
- And he believes in the death,
- And he believes in the Resurrection after death, and he believes in Al-Qadar [Jami` at-Tirmidhi, Vol. 4, Book 6, Hadith 2145]
- No person believes, till I am dearer to him than the members of his household, his wealth, and the whole of mankind. [Sahih Muslim, Book 1, Hadith 70]
- "Trials will not cease afflicting the believing man and the believing woman in their self, children, and wealth, until they meet Allah (SWT) without having any sin." [Jami` at-Tirmidhi, Vol. 4, Book 10, Hadith 2399]

3-Rewards of believers of Allah (SWT)

- He will **admit them to mercy** from Himself
- **Guide them** to Himself on a **straight path** [An-Nisa: 175]

- For it is expected that those will be of the [**rightly] guided**. [At-Tawbah: 18]

2 FEAR OF ALLAH (SWT)

It includes 19 ayah and 3 ahadith.

A-Ayah

171.**They receive good tidings of favour from Allah (SWT)** and bounty and [of the fact] that Allah (SWT) does not allow the reward of believers to be lost – 172.Those [believers] who responded to Allah (SWT) and the Messenger after injury had struck them. For those who **did good among them and feared Allah (SWT)** is a great reward – 186. You will surely be **tested in your possessions and in yourselves**. And you will surely hear from those who were given the Scripture before you and from those who associate others with Allah (SWT) much abuse. **But if you are patient and fear Allah (SWT) –indeed, that is of the matters [worthy] of determination. 198. But those who feared their Lord will have gardens beneath which rivers flow, abiding eternally therein, as accommodation from Allah (SWT). And that which is with Allah (SWT) is best for the righteous.** [Al-e-Imran: 171, 186, 198]

11.O you who have believed, remember the favor of Allah (SWT) upon you when a people determined to extend their hands [in aggression] against you, but He withheld their hands from you; and fear Allah

(SWT). And upon Allah (SWT) let the believers **rely on**. 28. If you should raise your hand against me to kill me −I shall not raise my hand against you to kill you. Indeed, I **fear Allah (SWT)**, Lord of the worlds. 57.O you who have believed, **take not** those who have taken your religion in ridicule and amusement among the ones who were given the Scripture before you nor the disbelievers as **allies**. And fear Allah (SWT), if you should [truly] be believers. 93. There is not upon those who believe and do righteousness [any] blame concerning what they have eaten [in the past] if they [now] fear Allah (SWT) and believe and do righteous deeds, and then **fear Allah (SWT)** and believe, and then fear Allah (SWT) and do good; and Allah (SWT) loves the doers of good. [Al-Maidah: 11, 28, 57, 93]

And those who **fear Allah (SWT) are not held accountable for them [i.e., the disbelievers]** at all, but [only for] a reminder −that perhaps they will fear Him. [Al-Anaam: 69]

And decree for us in this world [that which is] good and [also] in the Hereafter; indeed, we have turned back to You." [Allah (SWT)] said, "My punishment −I afflict with it whom I will, but My mercy encompasses all things." So, I will decree it [especially] for those who fear Me and give zakah and those who **believe in Our verses** − [Al-Aaraf: 156]

The believers are only those who, when Allah (SWT) is mentioned, **their hearts become fearful**, and when **His verses are recited to them, it** increases them in faith; and upon their Lord, they rely. [Al-Anfal: 2]

18. **The mosques of Allah (SWT) are only to be maintained** by those who **believe in Allah (SWT)** and the **Last Day and establish_prayer and give zakah and do not fear except Allah (SWT),** for it is expected that those will be of the [rightly] guided. 44. Those who believe in Allah (SWT) and the Last Day would **not ask permission of you to be excused from striving [i.e., fighting]** with their wealth and their lives. And Allah (SWT) is Knowing of those who fear Him. [At-Tawbah: 18, 44]

Indeed, in the alternation of the night and the day and [in] what Allah (SWT) has created in the heavens and the earth are signs for a people who **fear Allah (SWT).** 63.Those who believed and were **fearing Allah (SWT)** [Yunus: 6, 63]

And those who **join that which Allah (SWT) has ordered to be joined and fear their Lord and are afraid of the evil of [their] account,** [Ar-Raad: 21]

And it will be said to **those who feared Allah (SWT)**, "What did your Lord send down?" They will say, "[That which is] good." For those who do good in this world is good, and the home of the Hereafter is better. And how excellent is the home of the righteous? [An-Nahl: 30]
She said, "Indeed, I **seek refuge** in the Most Merciful from you, [so leave me] if you should be fearing of Allah (SWT). [Maryam: 18]

Who, **when Allah (SWT) is mentioned, their hearts are fearful**, and [to]the patient over what has afflicted them, and the establishers of prayer and those who spend from what We have provided them. [Al-Hajj: 35]

Indeed, they **who are apprehensive from fear of their Lord [Al-Muminun: 57]**

B-Ahadith

It was narrated that Abu Hurairah said: "No man who weeps for fear of Allah (SWT) will be touched by the Fire until the milk goes back into the udders. And the dust (of Jihad) in the cause of Allah (SWT) and the smoke of Hell, will never be combined in the nostrils of a Muslim." [Sunan an-Nasa'i, Vol. 1, Book 25, Hadith 3109]

Narrated Ali ibn AbuTalib: The last words which the Messenger of Allah (SWT) (⬥) spoke were: Prayer, prayer; fear Allah (SWT) about those whom your right hands possess. [Sunan Abi Dawud, Book 42, Hadith 5137]

On the authority of Abu Dharr Jundub ibn Junadah, and Abu Abdur-Rahman Muadh bin Jabal (may Allah (SWT) be pleased with him), that the Messenger of Allah (SWT) (peace and blessings of Allah (SWT) be upon him) said: Have taqwa **(fear) of Allah (SWT)** wherever you may be, and follow up a bad deed with a good deed which will wipe it out, and behave well towards the people. It was related by at-Tirmidhi, who said it was a hasan (good) hadeeth, and in some copies, it is stated to be a hasan saheeh hadeeth. [40 Hadith Nawawi, Hadith 18]

Abu Hurairah (RAA) narrated that the Messenger of Allah (SWT) (ﷺ) said: "The fear of Allah (SWT) and good morals (Akhlaq) are the two major characteristics which lead to Paradise." Related by At-Tirmidhi and Al-Hakim graded it as Sahih. [Bulugh al-Maram, Book 16, Hadith 1576]

Key points

1-Allah (SWT) commands to fear Him

And fear Allah (SWT), if you should [truly] be believers. [Al-Maidah: 11, 28, 57, 93]

Messenger of Allah (SWT) (peace and blessings of Allah (SWT) be upon him) said: **Have taqwa (fear) of Allah (SWT)** wherever you may be [40 Hadith Nawawi, Hadith 18]

2-Who fear Allah (SWT)?

- And those who **join** that which Allah (SWT) has ordered to be joined
- And **fear their Lord** and
- Are **afraid of the evil of [their] account**, [Ar-Raad: 21]
- **When Allah (SWT) is mentioned, their hearts are fearful**, [Al-Hajj: 35]
- Who are **apprehensive from fear of their Lord** [Al-Muminun: 57]?

3-Reward of those who fear Allah (SWT)

But those who feared their Lord will have

* **Gardens** beneath which rivers flow,
* Abiding eternally therein, as **accommodation** from Allah (SWT). [Al-e-Imran: 198]

Allah (SWT) loves the doers of good. [Al-Maidah: 93]

And those who fear Allah (SWT) are not held accountable for them [i.e., the disbelievers] at all, [Al-Anaam: 69]

But if you are patient and fear Allah (SWT) – indeed, **that is of the matters [worthy] of determination**. [Al-e-Imran: 198]

The messenger (SAW) of Allah (SWT) **"No man who weeps for fear of Allah (SWT) will be touched by the Fire** until the milk goes back into the udders. [Sunan an-Nasa'i, Vol. 1, Book 25, Hadith 3109]

3
RIGHTEOUSNESS

It includes 16 ayah and 3 ahadith.

They believe in Allah (SWT) and the Last Day, and they enjoin what is right and forbid what is wrong and hasten to good deeds. And those are among the righteous.[Al-e-Imran: 114]

And why should we not **believe in Allah (SWT) and what has come to us of the truth?** *And we aspire that our Lord will admit us [to Paradise] with the righteous people."* [Al-Maidah: 84]

There is not upon those who believe and do righteousness [any] blame concerning what they have eaten [in the past] if they [now] fear Allah (SWT) and believe and do righteous deeds, and then **fear Allah (SWT)** and believe, and then fear Allah (SWT) and do good; and Allah (SWT) loves the doers of good. [Al-Maidah: 93]

Righteousness is not that you turn your faces toward the east or the west, but [true] righteousness is [in] one who believes in Allah (SWT), the Last Day, the angels, the

Book, and the prophets and gives wealth, in spite of love for it, to relatives, orphans, the needy, the traveler, those who ask [for help], and for freeing slaves; [and who] establishes prayer and gives zakāh; [those who] fulfil their promise when they promise; and [those who] are patient in poverty and hardship and during battle. Those are the ones who have been true, and it is those who are righteous. [Al-Baqarah: 177]

Do not stand [for prayer] within it—ever. A mosque founded on righteousness from the first day is more worthy for you to stand in. Within it are men who love to *purify themselves*, and Allah (SWT) loves those who purify themselves. [At-Tawbah: 108]

And he who repents and does righteousness does indeed turn to Allah (SWT) with [accepted] repentance.[Al-Furqan: 71]

Whoever disbelieves – upon him is [the consequence of] his disbelief. And whoever does **righteousness** – they are for themselves preparing, [Ar-Rum: 44]

But they who believe and do **righteous deeds** – those are the *companions of Paradise*; they will abide therein eternally. [Al-Baqarah: 82] Indeed, those who **believe and do righteous deeds** and **establish prayer** and **give zakāh** will have their reward with their Lord, and there will be no fear concerning them, nor will they grieve. [Al-Baqarah: 277]

Allah (SWT)　　has promised those who have **believed among you and done righteous deeds** that He will surely *grant them succession [to authority] upon the earth* just as He granted it to those before them and that He will surely establish for them [therein] their religion which He has preferred for them and that He will surely *substitute for them, after their fear, security,* [for] **they worship Me, not associating anything with Me**. But whoever disbelieves after that −then those are defiantly disobedient. [An-Nur: 55]

Except for those who repent, believe and do righteous work. For them, Allah (SWT) will replace their evil deeds with good. And ever is Allah (SWT) Forgiving and Merciful [Al-Furqan:70]

And **those who believe and do righteous deeds** − We will surely remove from them their misdeeds and will surely reward them according to the best of what they used to do.[Al-Ankabut: 7]

And those who **believe and do righteous deeds** −We will surely *admit them among the righteous* [into Paradise]. [Al-Ankabut: 9]

That He may reward **those who believe and do righteous deeds**. Those will have forgiveness and **noble provision. [Saba: 4]**

So as for **those who believed and did righteous deeds**, their Lord will admit them into His mercy.

That is what is the clear attainment. [Al-Jathiyah/Jasia: 30]

And those who **believe and do righteous deeds** and believe in what has been sent down upon Muhammad–and it is the truth from their Lord –He will remove from them their misdeeds and amend their condition. [Surah Muhammad: 2]

No! Indeed, the **record of the righteous is in 'illiyyun**. [Al-Mutaffifeen: 18]

B-Ahadith

Abdullah bin Mas'ud narrated that the Messenger of Allah (SWT) said: "Abide by truthfulness. For indeed **truthfulness leads to righteousness**. And indeed, righteousness leads to Paradise. A man continues telling the truth and trying hard to tell the truth until he is recorded with Allah (SWT) as a truthful person. Refrain from falsehood. For indeed falsehood leads to wickedness, and wickedness leads to the Fire. A slave (of Allah (SWT)) continues lying and trying hard to lie, until he is recorded with Allah (SWT) as a liar." [Jami` at-Tirmidhi, Vol. 4, Book 1, Hadith 1971]

Narrated `Abdullah: Allah (SWT)'s Messenger (ﷺ) said, "Do not wish to be like anyone, except in two cases: (1) **A man whom Allah (SWT) has given wealth and he spends it righteously.** (2) A man whom Allah (SWT) has given wisdom (knowledge of the Qur'an and the Hadith) and he acts according to it and teaches it to others." [Al-Bukhari, Vol. 9, Book 89, Hadith 255]

Abu Huraira reported Allah (SWT)'s Messenger (ﷺ) as saying: **He who called (people) to righteousness, there would be reward (assured) for him like the rewards of those who adhered to it**, without their rewards being diminished in any respect. And he who called (people) to error, he shall have to carry (the burden) of its sin, like those who committed it, without their sins being diminished in any respect. [Sahih Muslim, Book 34, Hadith 6470]

Key points

1-Who are righteous?

- Believe in Allah (SWT) [Al-e-Imran: 114]
- Believe in the Last Day [Al-e-Imran: 114]
- Enjoin what is right and forbid what is wrong [Al-e-Imran: 114]
- Hasten to good deeds. [Al-e-Imran: 114]
- Believe in what has come to us of the truth? [Al-Maidah: 84]
- Fear Allah (SWT) [Al-Maidah: 93]
- Believes in Allah (SWT), the Last Day, the angels, the Book, and the prophets and gives wealth, in spite of love for it, to relatives, orphans, the needy, the traveller, those who ask [for help], and for freeing slaves; [and who] establishes prayer and gives zakāh; [those who] fulfil their promise when they promise; and [those who] are patient in poverty and hardship and during battle. Those are the ones who have been true, and it is those who are righteous. [Al-Baqarah: 177]

- Purify themselves [At-Tawbah: 108]
- Turn to Allah (SWT) with [accepted] repentance. [Al-Furqan: 71]
- They are for themselves preparing, [Ar-Rum: 44]
- Truthfulness leads to righteousness [Jami` at-Tirmidhi, Vol. 4, Book 1, Hadith 1971]
- A man whom Allah (SWT) has given wealth and he spend it righteously [Al-Bukhari, Vol. 9, Book 89, Hadith 255]

2-Reward of righteous people

- Companions of Paradise [Al-Baqarah: 82]
- No fear concerning, no grieve [Al-Baqarah: 277]
- Lord will guide them [Yunus: 9]
- Will have forgiveness [Hudh: 11]
- Grant them succession [to authority] upon the earth [An-Nur: 55]
- Substitute for them, after their fear, security [An-Nur: 55]
- Allah (SWT) will replace their evil deeds with good [Al-Furqan:70]
- Admit them among the righteous [Al-Ankabut: 9]
- We will surely remove from them their misdeeds [Al-Ankabut: 7]
- Those will have ... noble provision. [Saba: 4]
- Admit them into His mercy [Al-Jathiyah: 30]
- Amend their condition. [Surah Muhammad: 2]
- The record of the righteous is in 'illiyyun. [Al-Mutaffifeen: 18]
- He who called (people) to righteousness, there would be reward (assured) for him like the rewards of those who adhered to it [Sahih Muslim, Book 34, Hadith 6470]

4 PATIENCE

It includes 15 ayah and 3 ahadith.

A-Ayah

Righteousness is not that you turn your faces toward the east or the west, but [true] righteousness is [in] one who **believes in Allah (SWT)**, the **Last Day**, **the angels**, **the Book**, and **the prophets** and **gives wealth**, in spite of love for it, to relatives, orphans, the needy, the traveller, those who ask [for help], and for **freeing slaves**; [and who] **establishes prayer** and **gives zakāh**; [those who] **fulfil their promise** when they promise; and [those who] are *patient in poverty and hardship and during battle*. Those are the ones who have been **true**, and it is those who are **righteous**. [Al-Baqarah: 177]

Except for **those who are patient and do righteous deeds**; those will have forgiveness and great reward. [Hudh: 11]

And **those who are patient, seeking the countenance of their Lord, and establish prayer and spend from what We have provided for them secretly and publicly and prevent evil with good** – those will have the good consequence of [this] home [Ar-Raad: 22]

"And why should we not put our trust in Allah (SWT) while He indeed has guided us our ways. And we shall certainly bear with patience all the hurt you may cause us, and in Allah (SWT) (Alone) let those who trust, put their trust." [Ibraheem: 12]

[They are] **those who endured patiently and upon their, Lord relied on**. 96. Whatever you have will end, but what Allah (SWT) has is lasting. And We will surely give **those who were patient** their reward according to the best of what they used to do. [An-Nahl: 42, 96]

Then, indeed your Lord, to **those who emigrated after they had been compelled [to say words of disbelief] and thereafter fought [for the cause of Allah (SWT)] and were patient** – indeed, your Lord, after that, is Forgiving and Merciful. ? [An-Nahl: 110]

Who, **when Allah (SWT) is mentioned, their hearts are fearful**, *and [to] the patient over what has afflicted them*, and the establishers of prayer and those who spend from what We have provided them. [Al-Hajj: 35]

Indeed, I have rewarded them this Day for their **patient endurance** – that they are the attainers [of success]." [Al-Muminun: 111]

Those will be given their reward twice for what they **patiently** endured and [because] they **avert evil through good**, and from what We have provided them they **spend**.[Al-Qasas: 54]

Who has been **patient and upon their Lord rely on?** [Al-Ankabut: 59]

"O my son! Aqim-is-Salat (perform As-Salat), enjoin (people) for Al-Ma'ruf (Islamic Monotheism and all that is good), and forbid (people) from Al-Munkar (i.e. disbelief in the Oneness of Allah (SWT), polytheism of all kinds and all that is evil and bad), **and bear with patience whatever befall you.** Verily! These are some of the important commandments ordered by Allah (SWT) with no exemption. [Luqman: 17]

Indeed, the Muslim men and Muslim women, the believing men and believing women, the obedient men and obedient women, the truthful men and truthful women, the patient men and patient women, the humble men and humble women, the charitable men and charitable women, the fasting men and fasting women, the men who guard their private parts and the women who do so, and the men who remember Allah (SWT) often and the women who do so – for them **Allah (SWT) has prepared forgiveness and a great reward. [Al-Ahzab: 35]**

Say, "O My servants who have **believed, fear your Lord**. For those who do good in this world is good, and the earth of Allah (SWT) is spacious. Indeed, the patient will be given their reward without account [i.e., limit]." [A-Zumar: 10]

Except for those who have **believed and done righteous deeds and advised each other to**

truth and advised each other to patience.[Al-Asr: 3]

B-Ahadith

Abu Sa'id and Abu Hurairah (May Allah (SWT) be pleased with him) reported that the Prophet (ﷺ) said: "Never a believer is stricken with a discomfort, an illness, an anxiety, a grief or mental worry or even the pricking of a thorn but **Allah (SWT) will expiate his sins on account of his patience"**. [Book 1, Hadith 37]

Narrated Abu Sa`id: Some people from the Ansar asked Allah (SWT)'s Messenger (ﷺ) (to give them something) and he gave to every one of them, who asked him, until all that he had was finished. When everything was finished and he had spent all that was in his hand, he said to them, '"(Know) that if I have any wealth, I will not withhold it from you (to keep for somebody else); And (know) that he who refrains from begging others (or doing prohibited deeds), Allah (SWT) will make him contented and not in need of others; and he who remains patient, Allah (SWT) will bestow patience upon him, and he who is satisfied with what he has, **Allah (SWT) will make him self-sufficient.** And there is no gift better and vast (you may be given) than patience." [Al-Bukhari, Vol. 8, Book 76, Hadith 477]

Abu Hurairah (May Allah (SWT) be pleased with him) reported: The Messenger of Allah (SWT) (ﷺ) said: "Allah (SWT), the Exalted, says: 'I have no reward except Jannah for a believing slave of Mine who shows patience and anticipates My reward when

I take away his favourite one from the inhabitants of the world."' [Al-Bukhari, Book 7, Hadith 923]

Key points

The dictionary meaning of patience is "the capacity to accept or tolerate delay, problems, or suffering without becoming annoyed or anxious"[2]

1-What is patience?

- Patient in poverty and hardship and during battle. [Al-Baqarah: 177]
- And we shall certainly bear with patience all the hurt you may cause us, and in Allah (SWT) (Alone) let those who trust, put their trust." [Ibraheem: 12]
- *And [to] the patient over what has afflicted them,* [Al-Hajj: 35]
- For their patient endurance [Al-Muminun: 111]
- And bear with patience whatever befall you. [Luqman: 17]

2-Reward for parient people

- Great reward. [Hudh: 11]
- Those will have the good consequence of [this] home [Ar-Raad: 22]
- Forgiving (forgiveness and mercy) and merciful.? [An-Nahl:110]
- Attainers [of success]." [Al-Muminun: 111]
- Allah (SWT) has prepared forgiveness and a great reward. [Al-Ahzab: 35]

---

[2] https://www.lexico.com/en/definition/patience

- The patient will be given their reward without account [i.e., limit]." [Al-Zumar: 10]
- Allah (SWT) will expiate his sins on account of his patience". [Book 1, Hadith 37]
- Allah (SWT) will make him self-sufficient [Al-Bukhari, Vol. 8, Book 76, Hadith 477]
- 'I have no reward except Jannah for a believing slave of mine who shows patience [Al-Bukhari, Book 7, Hadith 923]

5 REPENT ALLAH (SWT)

It includes 7 ayah and 3 ahadith.

A-Ayah

The **repentance** accepted by Allah (SWT) is only for those who do wrong in ignorance [or carelessness] and then repent soon after. It is those to whom Allah (SWT) will turn in forgiveness, and Allah (SWT) is ever Knowing and Wise. [An-Nisa: 17]

Except for those who repent, correct themselves, hold fast to Allah (SWT), and are **sincere** in their religion for Allah (SWT), for those will be with the believers. And Allah (SWT) is going to give the believers a great reward. [An-Nisa: 146]

When those who believe in Our Ayat (proofs, evidences, verses, lessons, signs, revelations, etc.) come to you, say: "Salamun 'Alaikum" (peace be on you); your Lord has written Mercy for Himself, so that, *if any of you does evil in ignorance*, *and thereafter repents* and does righteous good deeds (by obeying Allah (SWT)), then surely, He is Oft-Forgiving, Most Merciful. [Al-Anaam: 54]

Except for those who _repent_, believe and do _righteous work_. For them, Allah (SWT) will replace their evil deeds with good. And ever is Allah (SWT) Forgiving and Merciful. [Al-Furqan: 70]

Then, indeed your Lord, to those who have done wrong out of ignorance and then **repent after that and correct themselves** – indeed, your Lord, thereafter, is Forgiving and Merciful. [An-Nahl: 119]

And he who repents and does righteousness does indeed turn to Allah (SWT) with [accepted] _repentance_.[Al-Furqan: 71]

Perhaps his Lord, if he divorced you [all], would substitute for him wives better than you – **submitting [to Allah (SWT)], believing, devoutly obedient, repentant, worshipping,** and **traveling** –[ones] previously married and virgins.[At-Tahreem: 5]

B-Ahadith

It was narrated from Abu Hurairah that the Prophet (🕮) said: "If you were to commit sin until your sins reach the heaven, then you were to repent, your repentance would be accepted." [Sunan Ibn Majah, Vol. 5, Book 37, Hadith 4248]

Narrated Mu'awiyah: I heard the Messenger of Allah (SWT) (🕮) say: Migration will not end until repentance ends, and repentance will not end until the sun rises in the west. [Sunan Abi Dawud, Book 14, Hadith 2473]

It was narrated that Ibn Ma'qil said: "I entered with my father upon 'Abdullah, and I heard him say: 'The messenger of Allah (SWT) (ﷺ) said: "Regret is repentance." My father said: 'Did you hear the Prophet (ﷺ) say: "Regret is repentance?" He said: 'Yes.'" [Sunan Ibn Majah, Vol. 5, Book 37, Hadith 4252]

Key points

It includes the following aspects.

1-What is repentance?

The Prophet said, "Regret is repentance." [Sunan Ibn Majah, Vol. 5, Book 37, Hadith 4252]
The dictionary meaning of repentance is to "Feel or express sincere regret or remorse about one's wrongdoing or sin." And "View or think of (an action or omission) with deep regret or remorse."[3]

2-Whose repentance is accepted?

- The repentance accepted by Allah (SWT) is only for those who do wrong in ignorance [or carelessness] and then repent soon after. [An-Nisa: 17]
- If any of you does evil in ignorance, and thereafter repents [Al-Anaam: 54]

---

[3]https://www.lexico.com/en/definition/patience

3-When repentance would end?

Repentance will not end until the sun rises in the west. [Sunan Abi Dawud, Book 14, Hadith 2473]

4-Reward of repentance

- Allah (SWT) is going to give the believers a great reward. [An-Nisa: 146]
- Allah (SWT) will replace their evil deeds with good. And ever is Allah (SWT) Forgiving and Merciful. [Al-Furqan: 70]
- "If you were to commit sin until your sins reach the heaven, then you were to repent, your repentance would be accepted." [Sunan Ibn Majah, Vol. 5, Book 37, Hadith 4248]

6 EMIGRATES FOR THE CAUSE OF ALLAH (SWT)

It includes 7 ayah and 3 ahadith.

A-Ayah

And whoever **emigrates** for the cause of **Allah (SWT) will find on the earth many [alternative] locations and abundance.** And whoever leaves his home as an emigrant to Allah (SWT) and His Messenger and then death overtakes him – his reward has already become incumbent upon Allah (SWT). And Allah (SWT) is ever Forgiving and Merciful. [An-Nisa: 100]

Indeed, those who have **believed and emigrated and fought** with their wealth and lives in the cause of Allah (SWT) and those who **gave shelter and aided** – they are allies of one another. But those who believed and did not emigrate – for you there is no support of them until they emigrate. And if they seek the help of you for the religion, then you must help, except against a people between yourselves and who is a treaty. And Allah (SWT) is Seeing of what you do. [Al-Anfal: 72]

The ones who have **believed, emigrated and striven in the cause of Allah (SWT) with their**

wealth and their lives are greater in rank in the sight of Allah (SWT). And it is those who are the attainers [of success]. [At-Tawbah: 20]

41. And **those who emigrated for [the cause of] Allah (SWT)** after they had been wronged –*We will surely settle them in this world in a good place*; but the reward of the Hereafter is greater, if only they could know. 110. Then, indeed your Lord, to **those who emigrated after they had been compelled [to say words of disbelief] and thereafter fought [for the cause of Allah (SWT)] and were patient** –indeed, your Lord, after that, is Forgiving and Merciful. ? [An-Nahl: 41, 110]

And those who emigrated for the cause of Allah (SWT) and then were **killed or died** – *Allah (SWT) will surely provide for them a good provision.* And indeed, it is Allah (SWT) who is the best of providers. [Al-Hajj: 58]

And [also for] those who were settled in the Home [i.e., al-Madinah] and [adopted] the faith before them. They **love those who emigrated** to them and find not any want in their breasts of what they [i.e., the emigrants] were given but give **[them] preference over themselves, even though they are in privation. And whoever is protected from the stinginess of his soul** – it is those who will be successful. [Al-Hashr: 9]

B-Ahadith

Narrated 'Abdullah bin 'Amr: The Prophet (ﷺ) said, "A Muslim is the one who avoids harming Muslims with his tongue and hands. And a Muhajir (emigrant) is the one who gives up (abandons) all what Allah (SWT) has forbidden." [Al-Bukhari, Vol. 1, Book 2, Hadith 10]

It was narrated from Ma'qil bin Yasar that the Messenger of Allah (SWT) (ﷺ) said: **"Worship during the time of bloodshed is like emigrating to me." [Sunan Ibn Majah, Vol. 5, Book 36, Hadith 3985]**

Narrated Anas: The Prophet (ﷺ) said, "O Allah (SWT)! There is no life worth living except the life of the Hereafter, so (please) make righteous the Ansar and the Emigrants." [Sahih al-Bukhari, Vol. 8, Book 76, Hadith 422]

Key points

Emigration means "departure from a place of abode, natural home, or country for life or residence elsewhere"[4]

1-Who is emigrant?

And a Muhajir (emigrant) is the one who gives up (abandons) all what Allah (SWT) has forbidden." [Al-Bukhari, Vol. 1, Book 2, Hadith 10]

---

[4]https://www.merriam-webster.com/dictionary/emigration

2-Rewards of migration

- Allah (SWT) will find on the earth many [alternative] locations and abundance. [An-Nisa: 100]
- attainers [of success]. [At-Tawbah: 20]
- We will surely settle them in this world in a good place [An-Nahl: 41]
- Forgiveness is for them [An-Nahl: 110]
- Allah (SWT) will surely provide for them a good provision. [Al-Hajj: 58]
- it is those who will be successful. [Al-Hashr: 9]
- "Worship during the time of bloodshed is like emigrating to me." [Sunan Ibn Majah, Vol. 5, Book 36, Hadith 3985]
- The Prophet (ﷺ) give dua to emigrants. He says, "O Allah (SWT)! There is no life worth living except the life of the Hereafter, so (please) make righteous the Ansar and the Emigrants." [Sahih al-Bukhari, Vol. 8, Book 76, Hadith 422]

7 Remember Allah (SWT)

It includes 11 ayah and 3 ahadith.

A-Ayah

He gives wisdom to whom He wills, and whoever has been given wisdom has certainly been given much good. **And none will remember except those of understanding.** [Al-Baqrah: 269]

135. And those who, when they commit an immorality or wrong themselves [by transgression], **remember Allah (SWT) and seek forgiveness for their sins** –and who can forgive sins except Allah (SWT)? – and [who] do not persist in what they have done while they know. **191. Who remember Allah (SWT) while standing or sitting or [lying] on their sides and give thought to the creation of the heavens and the earth, [saying], "Our Lord, You did not create this aimlessly; exalted are You [above such a thing]; then protect us from the punishment of the Fire.** [Al-e-Imran: 135, 191]

And this is the path of your Lord, [leading] straight. We have detailed the verses for a people who **remember**. [Al-Annam: 126]

Those who believe (in the Oneness of Allah (SWT) - Islamic Monotheism), and whose hearts find rest in the remembrance of Allah (SWT), Verily, in the **remembrance of Allah (SWT) do hearts find rest**. [Ar-Raad: 28]

[Are] **men whom neither <u>commerce nor sale distract</u> from the remembrance of Allah (SWT) and performance of prayer and giving of zakah. They fear a Day in which the hearts and eyes will [fearfully] turnabout**. [An-Nur: 37]

Indeed, the <u>Muslim</u> men and Muslim women, the <u>believing</u> men and believing women, <u>the obedient</u> men and obedient women, <u>the truthful</u> men and truthful women, the <u>patient</u> men and patient women, the <u>humble</u> men and humble women, the <u>charitable</u> men and charitable women, the <u>fasting</u> men and fasting women, the men who <u>guard their private parts</u> and the women who do so, and the men who <u>remember Allah (SWT)</u> often and the women who do so – for them Allah (SWT) has prepared forgiveness and a great reward. [Al-Ahzab: 35]

Is the one who is **devoutly obedient during periods of the night**, prostrating and standing [in prayer], **fearing the Hereafter** and **hoping for the mercy of his Lord**, [like one who does not]? Say, "Are those who know equal to those who do not know?" ***Only they will remember [who are] people of understanding.*** [Az-Zumar: 9]

Allah (SWT) has sent down the best statement: a consistent Book wherein is reiteration. The skins shiver therefrom of those who **fear their Lord**;

then their skins and their hearts relax at the **remembrance** [i.e., mention] of Allah (SWT). That is the guidance of Allah (SWT) by which He guides whom He wills. And one whom Allah (SWT) leaves astray –for him there is no guide. [Az-Zumar: 23]

Has the time not come for those who have believed that *their hearts should become humbly submissive at the remembrance of Allah (SWT)* and what has come down of the truth? And let them not be like those who were given the Scripture before, and a long period passed over them, so their hearts hardened, and many of them are defiantly disobedient. [Al-Hadheedh: 16]

9.O you who have believed, **when [the adhan] is called for the prayer on the day of Jumuah [Friday], then** *proceed to the remembrance of Allah (SWT) and leave the trade.* That is better for you if you only knew. 10. And when the prayer has been concluded, disperse within the land and **seek from the bounty of Allah (SWT)**, and **remember Allah (SWT) often** that you may succeed. [Al-Jumah: 9-10]

B-Ahadith

Abu Hurairah (May Allah (SWT) be pleased with him) reported: The Messenger of Allah (SWT) (ﷺ) said, "Allah (SWT) the Exalted says: 'I am as my slave expects me to be, and **I am with him when he remembers Me**. If he remembers Me inwardly, I will remember him inwardly, and if he remembers Me in an assembly, I will remember him in a better assembly (i.e., in the assembly of angels)." [Al-Bukhari and Muslim, Book 16, Hadith 1435]

Jabir (May Allah (SWT) be pleased with him) reported: I heard the Messenger of Allah (SWT) (ﷺ) saying, "The best way to celebrate the remembrance of Allah (SWT) is to say: La ilaha illAllah (there is no true god except Allah (SWT))." [At-Tirmidhi, Book 16, Hadith 1437]

Abu Hurairah (May Allah (SWT) be pleased with him) reported: The Messenger of Allah (SWT) (ﷺ) said, "The Mufarridun have gone ahead." He was asked, "Who are the Mufarridun?" He (ﷺ) replied, "Those men and women who frequently celebrate the remembrance of Allah (SWT)." [Sahih Muslim, Book 16, Hadith 1436]

Key points

It includes three aspects.

1-Command of Allah (SWT)

- Remember Allah (SWT) when azan for Jummah is called out [Al-Jumah: 9]
- Seek from the bounty of Allah (SWT) and remember Allah (SWT) often that you may succeed. [Al-Jumah: 10]

2-Who will remember Allah (SWT)?

- And none will remember except those of understanding. [Al-Baqrah: 269]
- Business activity does not distract them [An-Nur: 37]
- Only they will remember [who are] people of understanding [Az-Zumar: 9]

- Their hearts should become humbly submissive at the remembrance of Allah (SWT) [Al-Hadheedh: 16]

3-Rewards of remembrance

- Remembrance of Allah (SWT) does hearts find rest. [Ar-Raad: 28]
- Allah (SWT) has prepared forgiveness and a great reward for them. [Al-Ahzab: 35]
- Their skins and their hearts relax at the remembrance [i.e., mention] of Allah (SWT). [Az-Zumar: 23]
- Allah (SWT) is with those who remember Him [Al-Bukhari and Muslim, Book 16, Hadith 1435]
- Those who remember Allah (SWT) are successful (Mufarridun) [Sahih Muslim, Book 16, Hadith 1436]

8 TRUTHFULNESS

It includes 4 ayah and 3 ahadith.

A-B-Ayah

That **Allah (SWT) may reward the truthful** for their truth and punish the hypocrites if He wills or accept their repentance. Indeed, Allah (SWT) is ever Forgiving and Merciful. [Al-Ahzab: 24]

35. Indeed, the <u>Muslim</u> men and Muslim women, the <u>believing</u> men and believing women, <u>the obedient</u> men and obedient women, <u>the truthful</u> men and truthful women, the <u>patient</u> men and patient women, the <u>humble</u> men and humble women, the <u>charitable</u> men and charitable women, the <u>fasting</u> men and fasting women, the men who <u>guard their private parts</u> and the women who do so, and the men who <u>remember Allah (SWT)</u> often and the women who do so – for them Allah (SWT) has prepared forgiveness and a great reward. . [Al-Ahzab: 35]

The believers are only the ones who have **believed in Allah (SWT) and His Messenger** and then doubt not but strive with their properties and their lives in the cause of Allah (SWT). It is those who are truthful. [Hujrat: 15]

For the poor **emigrants** who were expelled from their homes and their properties, seeking bounty from Allah (SWT) and [His] approval and supporting Allah (SWT) and His Messenger, [there is also a share]. Those are truthful. [Al-Hasher: 8]

B-Ahadith

Ibn Mas'ud (May Allah (SWT) be pleased with him) reported: The Messenger of Allah (SWT) (ﷺ) said, **"Truth leads to piety and piety leads to Jannah.** *A man persists in speaking the truth till he is recorded with Allah (SWT) as a truthful man.* Falsehood leads to transgression and transgression leads to the Hellfire. A man continues to speak falsehood till he is recorded with Allah (SWT) as a great liar." [Al-Bukhari and Muslim, Book 18, Hadith 1542]

Abu Sufyan (May Allah (SWT) be pleased with him) reported, in course of his detailed narration about Heraclius when the latter questioned him about the teachings of the Prophet (ﷺ) He said that: He (ﷺ) told (us): "Worship Allah (SWT) Alone and do not associate a thing with Him; and give up all that your ancestors said. "He also commands us to perform Salat (prayers), to speak the truth, to observe modesty and to strengthen the ties of kinship. [Al-Bukhari and Muslim, Book 1, Hadith 56]

Abu Sa'id Al-Khudri (May Allah (SWT) be pleased with him) said: The Prophet (ﷺ) said, **"The dwellers of Jannah** will look at those in the upper abodes above them as you look at a shining star which remains in the eastern or western horizon;

such will be the difference in superiority which some of them have over others." The Messenger of Allah (SWT) (☺) was asked: "Will those be the dwellings of the Prophets which no one else will be able to reach?" He (☺) replied, "Yes, but by Him in Whose Hand my soul is! men who believed in Allah (SWT) and acknowledged the truthfulness of the Messengers will reach them." [Al-Bukhari and Muslim, Book 20, Hadith 1887]

Key points

1-Who are truthful?

- Emigrants [Al-Hasher: 8]
- Seeking bounty from Allah (SWT) and [His] approval [Al-Hasher: 8]
- Supporting Allah (SWT) and His Messenger, [there is also a share]. [Al-Hasher: 8]

2-Rewards for them

- Reward the truthful [Al-Ahzab: 24]
- Allah (SWT) has prepared forgiveness [Al-Ahzab: 35]
- Truth leads to piety and piety leads to Jannah [Al-Bukhari and Muslim, Book 18, Hadith 1542]
- A man persists in speaking the truth till he is recorded with Allah (SWT) as a truthful man. [Al-Bukhari and Muslim, Book 18, Hadith 1542]
- The dwellers of Jannah ... and acknowledged the truthfulness of the Messengers will reach them." [Al-Bukhari and Muslim, Book 20, Hadith 1887]
- Basic teaching of Islam [Al-Bukhari and Muslim, Book 1, Hadith 56]

9 TRUST/RELY ON ALLAH (SWT)

It includes 4 ayah and 3 ahadith.

A-Ayah

O you who believe! Remember the Favour of Allah (SWT) unto you when some people desired (made a plan) to stretch out their hands against you, but (Allah (SWT)) withheld their hands from you. So, fear Allah (SWT). **And in Allah (SWT) let believers put their trust**. [Al-Maidah: 11]

"And why should we not put our trust in Allah (SWT) while He indeed has guided us our ways. And we shall certainly bear with patience all the hurt you may cause us, and in Allah (SWT) (Alone) let those who trust, put their trust." [Ibraheem: 12]

And He will provide him from (sources) he never could imagine. **And whosoever puts his trust in Allah (SWT), then He will suffice him**. Verily, Allah (SWT) will accomplish his purpose. Indeed, Allah (SWT) has set a measure for all things. [At-Talaq: 3]

159. And by the Mercy of Allah (SWT), you dealt with them gently. And had you been severe and

harsh hearted, they would have broken away from about you; so, pass over (their faults), and ask (Allah (SWT)'s) Forgiveness for them; and consult them in the affairs. Then when you have taken a decision, put your trust in Allah (SWT), certainly, **Allah (SWT) loves those who put their trust (in Him).** [Al-e-Imran: 159]

B-Ahadith

'Umar bin Al-Khattab narrated that the Messenger of Allah (SWT) said: "If you were to rely upon Allah (SWT) with the required reliance, then He would provide for you just as a bird is provided for, it goes out in the morning empty, and returns full." [Jami` at-Tirmidhi, Vol. 4, Book 10, Hadith 2344]

Abu Sa'eed narrated: "The Messenger of Allah (SWT) said: 'How can I be comfortable when the one with the horn is holding it to his lip, his ears listening for when he will be ordered to blow, so he can blow.' It was as if that was very hard upon the Companions of the Prophet (ﷺ), so he said to them: 'Say: "**Allah (SWT) is sufficient for us and what a good protector He is, and upon Allah (SWT) we rely**." [Jami` at-Tirmidhi, Vol. 4, Book 11, Hadith 2431]

Abu Hurairah (May Allah (SWT) be pleased with him) reported: The Messenger of Allah (SWT) (ﷺ) said, "He who keeps a horse for Jihad purposes, having faith in Allah (SWT) and **relying on His Promise**, will find that its fodder, drink, droppings and urine will all be credited to him in his Scales on the Day of Resurrection." [Al- Bukhari, Book 12, Hadith 1330]

It was narrated from Jabir bin 'Abdullah that the Messenger of Allah (SWT) (ﷺ) took the hand of a leper and made him eat with him, and said: "Eat, with trust in Allah (SWT) **and reliance upon Allah (SWT).**" [Sunan Ibn Majah, English reference: Vol. 4, Book 31, Hadith 3542]

Key points

1-Allah (SWT) commands to trust Him

- And in Allah (SWT) let believers put their trust [Al-Maidah: 11]
- And in Allah (SWT) (Alone) let those who trust, put their trust." [Ibraheem: 12]
- Reliance upon Allah (SWT)." [Sunan Ibn Majah, English reference: Vol. 4, Book 31, Hadith 3542]

2-Who trust on Allah (SWT)?

Allah (SWT) is sufficient for us and what a good protector He is, and upon Allah (SWT) we rely." [Jami` at-Tirmidhi, Vol. 4, Book 11, Hadith 2431]

3-Rewards of Allah (SWT)

- And whosoever puts his trust in Allah (SWT), then He will suffice him [At-Talaq: 3]
- Allah (SWT) loves those who put their trust (in Him). [Al-e-Imran: 159]
- Allah (SWT) can give easy provision like He give to birds [Jami` at-Tirmidhi, Vol. 4, Book 10, Hadith 2344]

10 SEEK FORGIVENESS OF ALLAH (SWT)

It includes 8 ayah and 3 ahadith.

A-Ayah

Kind speech and forgiveness are better than charity followed by injury. And Allah (SWT) is Free of need and Forbearing. [Al-Baqarah: 263]

The Messenger has believed in what was revealed to him from his Lord, and [so have] the believers. All of them have believed in Allah (SWT) and His angels and His books and His messengers, [saying], "We make no distinction between any of His messengers." And they say, "We hear, and we obey. [We seek] Your forgiveness, our Lord, and to You is the [final] destination." [Al-Baqarah: 285]

The patient, the true, the obedient, those who spend [in the way of Allah (SWT)], and those who seek forgiveness before dawn. [Al-e-Imran: 17]

And those who, when they commit an immorality or wrong themselves [by transgression], remember Allah (SWT) and seek forgiveness for their sins – and who can forgive sins except Allah (SWT)? – and [who] do not persist in what they have done while they know. [Al-e-Imran: 135]

The repentance accepted by Allah (SWT) is only for those who do wrong in ignorance [or carelessness] and then repent soon after. It is those to whom Allah (SWT) will turn in forgiveness, and Allah (SWT) is ever Knowing and Wise. [An-Nisa: 17]

But whoever repents after his wrongdoing and reforms, indeed, Allah (SWT) will turn to him in forgiveness. Indeed, Allah (SWT) is Forgiving and Merciful. [Al-Maidah: 39]

Except for **those who are patient and do righteous deeds**; those will have forgiveness and great reward. [Hudh: 11]

Indeed, **those who lower their voices before the Messenger of Allah (SWT)** – they are the ones whose hearts Allah (SWT) has tested for righteousness. For them are forgiveness and great reward. [Hujrat: 3]

B-Ahadith

'Abdullah bin Busr said that: The Prophet (ﷺ) said: **"Glad tidings** to those who find a lot of seeking forgiveness in the record of their deeds." [Sunan Ibn Majah, Vol. 5, Book 33, Hadith 3818]

It was narrated from Abu Hurairah that: the Messenger of Allah (SWT) (saas) said: 'I seek the forgiveness of **Allah (SWT) and repent to Him**

one hundred times each day.' [Sunan Ibn Majah, Vol. 5, Book 33, Hadith 3815]

Abu Bakr narrated: That the Messenger of Allah (SWT) (ﷺ) said: "He who seeks forgiveness has not been persistent in sin, even if he does it seventy times in a day." [Jami` at-Tirmidhi, Vol. 6, Book 46, Hadith 3559]

Key points

1-Command of Allah (SWT)

Allah (SWT) recommends forgiveness [Al-Baqarah: 263]

2-Who seeks forgiveness?

- Believers seek forgiveness of Allah (SWT)
- And those who, when they commit an immorality or wrong themselves [by transgression] [Al-e-Imran: 135]
- The Prophet (ﷺ) seeks 100 times daily [Sunan Ibn Majah, Vol. 5, Book 33, Hadith 3815]

3-Who deserves forgiveness?

- Those who do wrong in ignorance [or carelessness] [An-Nisa: 17]
- Those who lower their voices before the Messenger of Allah (SWT) [Hujrat: 3]

4-Reward of seeking forgiveness

- Allah (SWT) forgives them [Al-Maidah: 39]
- Allah (SWT) promises great reward [Hudh: 11]

- Glad tidings from Allah (SWT) [Sunan Ibn Majah, Vol. 5, Book 33, Hadith 3818]
- Allah (SWT) forgives if you ask seventy times daily [Jami` at-Tirmidhi, Vol. 6, Book 46, Hadith 3559]

11 FORTY QUALITIES IN BRIEF

The following ayah describe the general qualities of pious people.

1. The obedient (to Allah (SWT) [Al-e-Imran: 17]
2. Those who spend [in the way of Allah (SWT)], [Al-e-Imran: 17]
3. The praisers [of Allah (SWT)], [Al-e-Imran: 112]
4. The travellers [for His cause], those who bow and prostrate [in prayer], [Al-e-Imran: 112]
5. Those who enjoin what is right and forbid what is wrong, [Al-e-Imran: 112]
6. And those who observe the limits [set by] Allah (SWT) [Al-e-Imran: 112]
7. And give good tidings to the believers. [At-Tawbah: 112]
8. The Muslim men and Muslim women,
9. The believing men and believing women,
10. The obedient men and obedient women,
11. The truthful men and truthful women,
12. The patient men and patient women,
13. The humble men and humble women,
14. The charitable men and charitable women,
15. The fasting men and fasting women,
16. The men who guard their private parts and

17. The women who do so, and

18. The men who remember Allah (SWT) often and

19. The women who do so [Al-Ahzab: 35 from 8-19]

20. Those who avoid the major sins and immoralities, only [committing] slight ones. [An-Najum: 32]

21. And the slaves of the Most Beneficent (Allah (SWT)) are those who walk on the earth in humility and sedateness, (Al-Furqan: 63)

22. And when the foolish address them (with bad words) they reply back with mild words of gentleness. (Al-Furqan: 63)

23. And those who spend the night before their Lord, prostrate and standing. (Al-Furqan: 64)

24. And those who say: "Our Lord! Avert from us the torment of Hell. Verily! Its torment is ever an inseparable, permanent punishment.". (Al-Furqan: 65)

25. And those, who, when they spend, are neither extravagant nor niggardly, but hold a medium (way) between those (extremes). (Al-Furqan: 67)

26. And those who invoke not any other ilah (god) along with Allah (SWT), (Al-Furqan: 68)

27. Nor kill such life as Allah (SWT) has forbidden, except for just cause, (Al-Furqan: 68)

28. Nor commit illegal sexual intercourse (Al-Furqan: 68)

29. And those who do not witness falsehood, (Al-Furqan: 72)

30. And if they pass by some evil play or evil talk, they pass by it with dignity. (Al-Furqan: 72)

31. And those who, when they are reminded of the Ayat (proofs, evidences, verses, lessons, signs, revelations, etc.) Of their Lord, fall not deaf and blind thereat. (Al-Furqan: 73)

32. And those who say: "Our Lord! Bestow on us from our wives and our offspring who will be the comfort of our eyes and make us leaders for the Muttaqoon" (Al-Furqan: 74). "

33. Except those devoted to Salat (prayers) (Al-Maarij: 22)

34. 23. Those who remain constant in their Salat (prayers); (Al-Maarij: 23)

35. And those who guard their Salat (prayers) well, (Al-Maarij: 34)

36. And those in whose wealth there is a known right, ... beggar who asks, and for the unlucky (Al-Maarij: 24-25)

37. And those who believe in the Day of Recompense, (Al-Maarij: 26)

38. And those who fear the torment of their Lord, (Al-Maarij: 27)

39. And those who stand firm in their testimonies; (Al-Maarij: 33)

40. Seeking the good Pleasure of Allah (SWT) (An-Nisa: 114)

Appendix 1 Additional ayah about Righteousness

The appendix includes 28 ayahs.

And as for those who **believed and did righteous deeds**, He will give them in full their rewards and grant them extra from His bounty. But as for those who disdained and were arrogant, He will punish them with a painful punishment, and they will not find for themselves besides Allah (SWT) any protector or helper. [An-Nisa: 173]

But those who **believed and did righteous deeds** –We charge no soul except [within] its capacity. Those are the companions of Paradise; they will abide therein eternally. [AL-Aaraf: 42]

Indeed, those who have believed and done righteous deeds –their **Lord will guide them** because of their faith. Beneath them, rivers will flow in the Gardens of Pleasure. [Yunus: 9] Except for **those who are patient and do righteous deeds**; those will have forgiveness and great reward. [Hudh: 11]

Indeed, they **who have believed and done righteous deeds and humbled themselves to their Lord**–those are the companions of Paradise; they will abide eternally therein. [Hudh: 23]

And those who have **believed and done righteous deeds** –We will surely assign to them of Paradise [elevated] chambers beneath which rivers flow, wherein they abide eternally. Excellent is the reward of the [righteous] workers [Al-Ankabut: 58]

And as for those who had believed and done righteous deeds, they will be in a garden [of Paradise], delighted. [Ar-Rum: 15]

Indeed, those who **believe and do righteous deeds** – for them are the Gardens of Pleasure, [Luqman: 8]

As for those who **believed and did righteous deeds**, for them will be the Gardens of Refuge as accommodation for what they used to do. [As-Sajdah: 19]

Those who disbelieve will have a severe punishment, and those who **believe and do righteous deeds** will have forgiveness and great reward. [Al-Fatir: 7]

Indeed, those who **believe and do righteous deeds** –for them is a reward uninterrupted. [Ha-Meem-Sajdhah/Fusilat: 8]

22. You will see the wrongdoers fearful of what they have earned, and it will [certainly] befall them. And those who have **believed and done righteous deeds** will be in lush regions of the gardens [in Paradise] having whatever they will in the presence of their Lord. That is what is the great bounty. 23. It is that of which Allah (SWT) gives good tidings to His servants who **believe and do righteous deeds**. Say, [O Muhammad], "I do not ask you for it [i.e., this message] any payment [but] only good will through

[i.e., due to] kinship." And whoever commits a good deed −We will increase for him good therein. Indeed, Allah (SWT) is Forgiving and Appreciative. [Ash-Shura: 22-23]

Indeed, Allah (SWT) will admit those who have **believed and done righteous deeds** to gardens beneath which rivers flow, but those who disbelieve enjoy themselves and eat as grazing livestock eat, and the Fire will be a residence for them. [Surah Muhammad: 12]

Muhammad is the Messenger of God; and those with him are **forceful against the disbelievers, merciful among themselves**. You see them bowing and prostrating [in prayer], seeking bounty from **God and [His] pleasure. Their mark [i.e., sign] is on their faces [i.e., foreheads] from the trace of prostration. That is their description in the Torah. And their description in the Gospel is as a plant which produces its offshoots and strengthens them so they grow firm and stand upon their stalks, delighting the sowers - so that He [i.e., God] may enrage by them the disbelievers. God has promised those who believe and do righteous deeds among them forgiveness and a great reward.** [Al-Fatah: 29]

Indeed, those who have **believed and done righteous deeds** will have gardens beneath which rivers flow. That is the great attainment. [Al-Buruj: 11]

Except for those who **believe and do righteous deeds**, for they will have a reward uninterrupted. [At-Teen: 6]

Except for those who have **believed and done righteous deeds and advised each other to truth and advised each other to patience. [Al Asr: 3]**

Indeed, those who believed and those who were Jews or Christians or Sabeans [before Prophet Muhammad (ﷺ)] –those [among them] who **believed in Allah (SWT)** and the **Last Day** and **did righteousness** – will have their reward with their Lord, and no fear will there be concerning them, nor will they grieve. [Al-Baqarah: 62]

Indeed, those who have believed [in Prophet Muhammad (ﷺ)] and those [before him (ﷺ)] who were Jews or Sabeans or Christians –those [among them] who **believed in Allah (SWT) and the Last Day and did righteousness** –no fear will there be concerning them, nor will they grieve. [Al-Maidah: 69]

37. And it is not your wealth or your children that bring you nearer to Us in position, but it is [by being] one who has **believed and done righteousness**. For them, there will be a double reward for what they did, and they will be in the upper chambers [of Paradise], safe [and secure] [Saba: 37]

And those who are guided —He increases them in guidance and gives them their righteousness. [Al-Fatah: 17]

Indeed, those who **lower their voices before the Messenger of Allah (SWT)** – they are the ones whose hearts Allah (SWT) has tested for righteousness. For them are forgiveness and great reward [Hujrat: 3]

Then is one who laid the foundation of his building on righteousness [with fear] from Allah (SWT) and [seeking] His approval better or one who laid the foundation of his building on the edge of a bank about to collapse, so it collapsed with him in to the fire of Hell? And Allah (SWT) does not guide the wrongdoing people. [At-Tawbah: 109]

BIBLIOGRAPHY

Adair, John (2010) The Leadership of Muhammad (PBUH), New Delhi: Kogan Page India Private Limited.

Al-Bahaqi, Abi Bakker Ahmad Al-Hussain (2009) Dhalail Al-Nabuwwa, Karachi: Dharul Ishaat.

Allen, Louis A. (1958) Management and organization, New York: McGraw-Hill.

Chesbrough, H. W. "The era of open innovation." MIT Sloan Management Review 44, no. 3 (2003a): 35-41.

Chesbrough, H. W. Open Innovation: The New Imperative for Creating and Profiting from Technology. (Boston: Harvard Business Press, 2003b)

Chesbrough, H. W. 2006. "The era of open innovation." In Managing Innovation and Change, edited by David Moyle, 127-138. London: Sage Publications Ltd.

DeCenzo, David A. and Stephen P. Robbins (2010) Human Resource Management, New York: John Wiley & Sons.

Dess, Gregory G., G. T. Lumpkin, Alan B. Eisner (2006) Strategic Management: Text and Cases, New York: Irwin/McGraw-Hill.

Dyck, B and Mitchell J Neubert (2009) Principal of Management, South-Western.

Fulop, L, and S Linstead (1999) Management, A critical text, London: Macmillan.

Gilani, Mnazar Ahsan Gilani (1936) Al-Nabi Al-Khatam SallAllah o Alaihay Wasallam (Urdu), Jayyad Barqi Press: Dehli.

Haimann, Theo and Raymond L. Hilgert (1972) Supervision: Concepts and Practices of Management, South-Western Publishing Company.

Hameed Ullah, M. (2006) The Prophet's (ﷺ) Establishing a State and his Succession, Beacon Books: Lahore.

Haykal, Muhammad Husayn, Translated by Isma'il Razi A. al-Faruqi, The Life of Muhammad (ﷺ)http://www.witness-pioneer.org/vil/Books/MH_LM/default.htm

Ibn Ishaq Sirat Rasoul Allah (SWT), An abridged version, https://ia800206.us.archive.org/12/items/Sirat-lifeOfMuhammad By-ibnIshaq/SiratIbnIahaqInEnglish.pdf

Iqbal, Javed and Muhammad Mushtaq Ahmad (2009) Planning in the Islamic Tradition: The Case of Hijrah Expedition, INSIGHTS 01(3), 37-68.

Kaandhlawi, Muhammad Zakarya (1997), Fazail-e-Amaal, Lahore: Kutibkhana Faizi.

Kaandhlawi, Muhammad Yusaf (2012), Hayatus Sahabah, Delhi: Islamic Books Services.

Koontz, Harold, and Heinz Weihrich (2006) Essentials of Management, New Delhi: Tata McGraw-Hill Education, pp. 81-84.

Kreitner, R (2009) Principal of Management, South-Western.

Lais, Muhammad A (2018) Muhammad (ﷺ): A real Model for World Peace, Kemp House, 152-160 City Road, London, EC1 V2N.

Lings, M (1994) Muhammad, his life based on the earliest sources, Lahore: Suhail Academy.

Mayo, E. (1933), The Human Problems of an Industrial Organization, McMillan, New York, NY.

Mubarakpuri, Safiur Rahman (1995) "The Sealed Nectar" (Ar-Raheeq Al-Makhtum), Lahore: Al-Maktba Alsalfia.

Muhammad ibn Ishaq, (2004) The Life of Muhammad, Oxford University Press, Karachi.

Nadvi, Sulaiman Hussaini (2205) Khutbat-e-Seerat, Karachi: Zam-Zam Publishers.

Noamani, Shibli and Syed Solaiman Nadhvi (2004) Seeratun-Nabi, Karachi: Dharul-Ishaat.

Pea, Roy D. (2015) What Is Planning Development the Development of? Accessed: April 2015, http://web.stanford.edu/~roypea/RoyPDF%20folder/A11_Pea_82d.pdf

Peter H. Langford, Cameron B. Dougall, Louise P. Parkes, (2017) "Measuring leader behaviour: evidence for a "big five" model of leadership", Leadership & Organization Development Journal, Vol. 38 Issue: 1, pp.126-144, https://doi.org/10.1108/LODJ-05-2015-0103

Phalwari, Muhammad Jaafer (1995) Peghambr-e-Insaniat, Lahore: Idara Sakafat-e-Islamia.

Razi, Muhammad Wali (1987) Hadhi-e-Alam, Dharul-Ilm: Karachi.

Robbins, Stephen, and Mary Coulter (2017) Management, New Delhi: Pearson Education.

Saani, Javed Iqbal (2017) Prophet (ﷺ) Muhammad (ﷺ) as a planning expert, London: Intellectual Capital Enterprise Limited.

Saani, Javed Iqbal (2016) Responsibilities of Managers: Selected Ahadith, available on amazon.co.uk. (Paperback edition)

Schumpeter, J. A. (1934). *Theory of Economic Development*. Cambridge, MA: Harvard University Press.

Shoqi, Abu Khalil (2002) Atlas-Seerat-e-Nabvi, Darussalam: Lahore.

Siddiqi, Naeem (1997) The Benefactor of Humanity (Mohsin-e-Insaniyat), Dehli: Markazi Matabah Islami Publishers.

Smith, Mike (2007) Fundamentals of Management, Berkshire: McGraw Hill Education.

Stogdill, R.M. (1957), Leader Behaviour: Its Description and Measurement, Bureau of Business Research, College of Commerce and Administration, Ohio State University, Columbus.

Time Management Guide (2015) What is planning and why you need to plan, Accessed: April 2015, http://www.time-management-guide.com/planning.html

Books of Ahadith

Imam Muhammad ibn Isma`il al-Bukhari al-Ju`fi (1983) Sahih Al-Bukhari, Translated by Muhammad Muhsin Khan, Lahore: Kazi Publications.

Imâm Abut Hussain Muslim bin al-Hajjaj, SahIh Muslim, Translated by Nasiruddin al-Khattab, Riyadh, 2007, Maktaba Dar-us-Salam.

Imam Muslim ibn al-Ḥajjāj al-Qushayrī (1971-75) Translated by Abdul Hameed Siddiqui Sahih Muslim, Lahore, Sh. Muhammad Ashraf.

lmâm Hâfiz Abu Dawud, Sunan Abu Dawud Sulaiman bin Ash'ath, Maktaba Dar-us-Salam, Riyadh, 2007.

Imäm Hãfiz Abü 'Elsa Mohammad Ibn 'Elsa At-Tirmidhi, Jamia' At-Tirmıdhi, English Translation by Abu Khaliyl, Riyadh, 2007, Maktaba Dar-us-Salam.

Imiim Hiifiz Abu Abdur Rahmiin Ahmad bin Shu'aib bin 'Ali An-Nasa'i, Sunan An-Nasa'i, Riyadh, 2007, Maktaba Dar-us-Salam.

Imam Muhammad Bin Yazeed Ibn Majah Al-Qazwinf, Sunan Ibn Majah Translated by Nasiruddin al-Khattab, Riyadh, 2007, Maktaba Dar-us-Salam.

Abu Zakaria Al-Nawawi, Riyad-us-Saliheen, Riyadh, 2007, Maktaba Dar-us-Salam.

Imam Malik bin Ans (رضي الله عنه), Muwatta Imam Malik, translated in Urdu by Allama Molana Abdul Hakeem Akhtar Shahjahanpuri, Lahore: Fareed Book Stall, accessed on 14 November 2017, https://readingpk.com/muwatta-imam-malik-imam-muhammad-malik/
https://www.sunnah.com

INDEX

88

89

Other Books by the Author (S)

1. Prof Dr. Javed Iqbal Saani (2019) Strategic Management: The Approach of the Prophet (PBUH), Intellectual Capital Enterprise Limited, London, available on Amazon (Paperback edition)

2. Prof Dr. Javed Iqbal Saani (2019) Greatness of Allah (SWT) in the Words of Allah (SWT), Intellectual Capital Enterprise Limited, London, available on Amazon (Paperback edition)

3. Prof Dr. Javed Iqbal Saani (2019) Managerial Implications of the Major Expeditions of the Prophet [PBUH], Intellectual Capital Enterprise Limited, London, available on Amazon (Paperback edition)

4. Prof Dr. Javed Iqbal Saani (2019) Managerial Implications of the Major Military Expeditions of the Prophet [PBUH], Intellectual Capital Enterprise Limited, London, available on Amazon (Paperback edition)

5. Prof Dr. Javed Iqbal Saani (2019) Managerial Implications of the Major Non-Military Expeditions of the Prophet [PBUH], Intellectual Capital Enterprise Limited, London, available on Amazon (Paperback edition)

6. Prof Dr. Javed Iqbal Saani (2019) Managerial Implications of the Battle of Trench, Intellectual

Capital Enterprise Limited, London, available on Amazon (Paperback edition)

7. Prof Dr. Javed Iqbal Saani (2019) Managerial Implications of the Conquest of Makkah, Intellectual Capital Enterprise Limited, London, available on Amazon (Paperback edition)

8. Prof Dr. Javed Iqbal Saani (2019) Management Information Systems, Intellectual Capital Enterprise Limited, London, available on Amazon (Paperback edition)

9. Prof Dr. Javed Iqbal Saani (2019) Managerial Implications of the Battle of Hunain, Intellectual Capital Enterprise Limited, London, available on Amazon (Paperback edition)

10. Prof Dr. Javed Iqbal Saani (2019) Managerial Implications of the Battle of Uhadh Campaign, Intellectual Capital Enterprise Limited, London, available on Amazon (Paperback edition)

11. Prof Dr. Javed Iqbal Saani (2019) Tablighi Mazaakry, Intellectual Capital Enterprise Limited, London, available on Amazon (Paperback edition)

12. Prof Dr. Javed Iqbal Saani (2019) Managerial Implications of the Tabuk Campaign, Intellectual Capital Enterprise Limited, London, available on Amazon (Paperback edition)

13. Prof Dr. Javed Iqbal Saani (2019) Management Practices of the Prophet (ﷺ), Intellectual Capital Enterprise Limited, London, available on Amazon (Paperback edition)

14. Prof Dr. Javed Iqbal Saani (2018) Managerial Implications of the Hijrah Expedition, Intellectual Capital Enterprise Limited, London, available on Amazon (Paperback edition)

15. Prof Dr. Javed Iqbal Saani (2018) Managerial Implications of the Battle of BADR, Intellectual Capital Enterprise Limited, London, available on Amazon (Paperback edition)

16. Prof Dr. Javed Iqbal Saani (2018) Managerial Thoughts of the Prophet (ﷺ), Intellectual Capital Enterprise Limited, London, available on Amazon (Paperback edition)

17. Prof Dr. Javed Iqbal Saani (2018) Controlling Strategy of the Prophet (ﷺ), Intellectual Capital Enterprise Limited, London, available on Amazon (Paperback edition)

18. Prof Dr. Javed Iqbal Saani (2018) Leading Strategy of the Prophet (ﷺ), Intellectual Capital Enterprise Limited, London, available on Amazon (Paperback edition)

19. Prof Dr. Javed Iqbal Saani (2018) Organising Strategy of the Prophet (ﷺ), Intellectual Capital Enterprise Limited, London, available on Amazon (Paperback edition)

20. Prof Dr. Javed Iqbal Saani (2018) Planning Strategy of the Prophet (ﷺ), Intellectual Capital Enterprise Limited, London, available on Amazon (Paperback edition)

21. Prof Dr. Javed Iqbal Saani (2018) Qualities of Momins: The Quranic Perspective, Intellectual Capital Enterprise Limited, London, available on Amazon (Paperback edition)

22. Prof Dr. Javed Iqbal Saani (2018) Hajj Experience: Combining Dawah and Manasiks, Intellectual Capital Enterprise Limited, London, available on Amazon (Paperback edition)

23. Prof Dr. Javed Iqbal Saani (2018) Sukhn-e-Saani (The book of poetry), Intellectual Capital

Enterprise Limited, London, available on Amazon (Paperback edition)

24. Prof Dr. Javed Iqbal Saani (2018) Managing Your Projects, Intellectual Capital Enterprise Limited, London, available on amazon.co.uk. (Paperback edition)

25. Prof Dr. Javed Iqbal Saani (2017) Business Case Studies, Intellectual Capital Enterprise Limited, London, available on Amazon (Paperback edition)

26. Prof Dr. Javed Iqbal Saani (2017) Virtues of Sickness: Selected Ahadith, available on Amazon (Paperback edition)

27. Prof Dr. Javed Iqbal Saani (2017) Prophet (ﷺ) Muhammad (ﷺ) as a planning expert, available on Amazon (Paperback edition)

28. Prof Dr. Javed Iqbal Saani (2017) Muhammad (ﷺ): His Trials & Tribulations, available on Amazon (Paperback edition)

29. Prof Dr. Javed Iqbal Saani (2017) Sales and Marketing: Selected Ahadith, available on amazon.co.uk. (Paperback edition)

30. Prof Dr. Prof Dr. Javed Iqbal Saani (2016) Research Proposals: Contents & Exemplars, available on amazon.co.uk. (Paperback edition)

31. Prof Dr. Javed Iqbal Saani (2016) Responsibilities of Managers: Selected Ahadith, available on amazon.co.uk. (Paperback edition)

32. Prof Dr. Javed Iqbal Saani (2016) Experience: The Journey of My Life, available on amazon.co.uk. (Paperback edition)

33. Prof Dr. Javed Iqbal Saani (2012) Understanding Information Systems, Manchester: GRaASS.

34. Prof Dr Javed Iqbal Saani (2011) Digital Divide in South Asia ISBN: 9789699578120.
35. Prof Dr. Javed Iqbal Saani and Muhammad Rafi Khattak (2011) Managing Risk in Projects, ISBN: 9789699578090.
36. Prof Dr. Javed Iqbal Saani and Muhammad Nadeem Khan (2011, 2018) Understanding Project Management, ISBN: 978969957845, available on Amazon (Paperback edition)
37. Prof Dr. Javed Iqbal Saani (2011) Information Systems for Managers, Grass Books, Manchester.
38. Prof Dr. Javed Iqbal Saani (2010) Managing strategic change: a real-world case study, ISBN: 978-3838330952, available on amazon.co.uk. (Paperback edition)

[Please see the images of these books on the following pages in addition to my doctoral thesis]

Islamic Management Style

Managerial
Implications
of the
Non Military
Expeditions of the
PROPHET(PBUH)

First Edition 2010

Prof Javed Iqbal Saani, PhD

Prophet
Muhammad
[PBUH]as a
Planning Expert

Prof Javed Iqbal Saani, PhD

Organising & Strategy of the Prophet [PBUH]
Prof Javed Iqbal Saani, PhD

Leading Strategy of the Prophet [PBUH]
Prof Javed Iqbal Saani, PhD

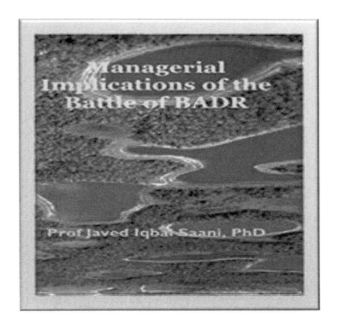

104

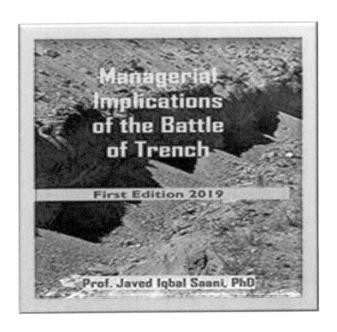

Management Sciences

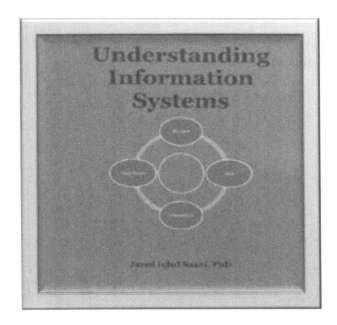

General Interest

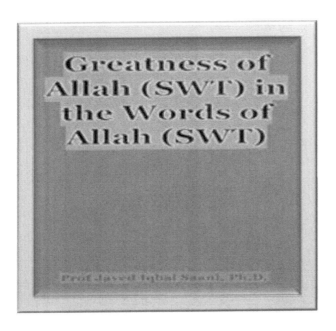

Greatness of Allah (SWT) in the Words of Allah (SWT)

Prof Javed Iqbal Saani, Ph.D.

Muhammad His Trials & Tribulations

Prof Javed Iqbal Saani, PhD

NOTES

Printed in Great Britain
by Amazon